FASCINATING FACTS ABOUT
The Solar System

By Jane Walker

Illustrated by Ian Thompson Cartoons by Tony Kenyon

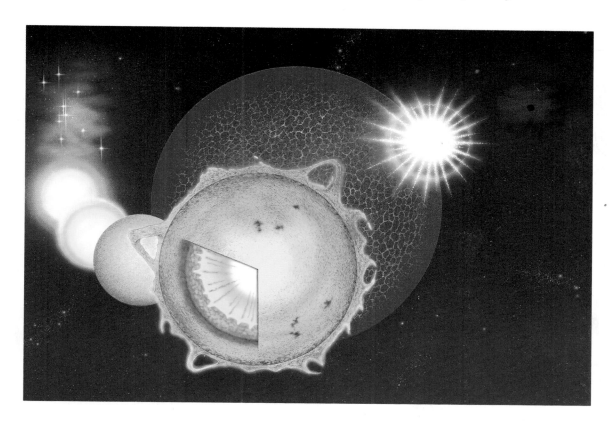

The Millbrook Press
Brookfield, Connecticut

INTRODUCTION

© 1994 Aladdin Books Ltd
Produced by Aladdin Books Ltd.
London W1P 9FF
Designed by David West
Children's Book Design

First published in
Great Britain in 1994 by
Watts Books, London

Published in the United States 1995
by The Millbrook Press
2 Old New Milford Road
Brookfield, Connecticut 06804

Printed in Belgium
Library of Congress Cataloging-in-
Publication Data
Walker, Jane (Jane Alison)
The solar system / by Jane Walker;
illustrated by Ian Thompson; cartoons by
Tony Kenyon.
p. cm. – (Fascinating facts about)
Includes index.
ISBN 1-56294-609-9 (lib.bdg.)
       1-56294-899-7 (pbk.)
1. Solar system – Juvenile literature. 2.
Astronomy – Juvenile literature. [1. Solar
system. 2. Astronomy.] I. Thompson,
Ian, 1964- ill. II. Kenyon, Tony, ill. III.
Title. IV. Series: Walker, Jane (Jane
Alison). Fascinating Facts.
Q8501.3.W35 1993   94-24597
523.2 – dc20   CIP AC

Did you know that the Earth is one of nine planets that circle around the sun? These planets, and everything else that travels around the sun, make up the solar system. In this book you can find out lots of interesting facts about the sun and its planets. You can also learn about shooting stars, moons, and what you can see in the night sky. Have fun doing our Solar System Quiz, and discover some Fascinating Facts about the solar system.

CONTENTS

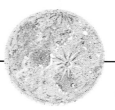

ORIGINS OF THE SOLAR SYSTEM

About 4.6 billion years ago, the solar system started to form. The sun was the first part to be made, followed later by the planets. The sun was made from giant clouds of dust and gas up in space. These clouds eventually pulled together, or condensed, becoming smaller, hotter, and brighter until finally the sun was formed.

Galaxies

Galaxies are huge families of stars up in space. The solar system is a tiny part of a galaxy called the Milky Way. With the help of very powerful telescopes, scientists have discovered that there are millions of other galaxies in space.

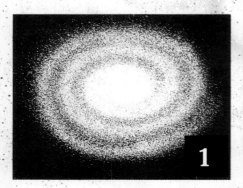

1

2

3

The stages

1. A huge, swirling cloud of gas and dust spinning around in space.
2. Pieces of rock and dust in the center of the cloud pulled inward to form a glowing ball of hot gases – the sun.
3. A leftover ring of dust and gas circled around the newly formed sun.

4. Over millions of years, the gas and dust in this ring stuck together, eventually forming the planets.

The Milky Way

Our galaxy, the Milky Way, is probably three times as old as the solar system. From the side, it looks like a thin, flat disc with a bulge in the middle. If you looked at it from above, it would look like a spiral. The sun and the rest of the solar system lie out toward the edge of the Milky Way (as shown above). On a clear, dark night the Milky Way can be seen as a faint band of white light across the sky.

4

All of the PLANETS in the solar system travel around the sun in the same direction in regular circles, called orbits.

WHAT IS THE SOLAR SYSTEM?

MERCURY

VENUS

EARTH

MARS

The word "solar" means anything to do with the sun. The solar system is made up of nine planets that all circle around, or orbit, the sun. It measures more than 7.5 billion miles across, and is shaped like a flat disc. Smaller objects – like moons, asteroids, comets, dust, and small rocks – are also part of the solar system.

The planets

After the sun, the largest objects in the solar system are the nine planets (although one of Saturn's moons is bigger than Mercury). Starting with the nearest planet to the sun, they are: Mercury, Venus, Earth, Mars, Jupiter, Saturn, Uranus, Neptune, and Pluto. Although Mercury is the closest to the sun, it is still 36 million miles away. The smallest planet, Pluto, is the farthest away from the sun. It is about 3,666 million miles away.

JUPITER

Make a planet mobile

Trace the planets from this page onto stiff cardboard and cut them out. To make the sun, attach a large semi-circle of cardboard to a wire coat-hanger. Color the sun and planets. Use string to hang each planet to the coathanger. Make pieces of string different lengths according to how far the planets are from the sun – Mercury will be on the shortest length, Pluto on the longest.

SATURN

URANUS

NEPTUNE

PLUTO

THE SUN

The sun is a huge ball of very hot gases. The temperature at its center can be as hot as 27 million degrees Fahrenheit (°F). The sun is much bigger than any of the planets in the solar system. It gives off enormous amounts of energy. Some of this energy comes to earth as heat and light.

Core of HELIUM and HYDROGEN gases

Birth

The sun was formed from clouds of dust and gas in space (see page 5). At its center, or core, millions of tons of a gas called hydrogen are turned into another gas called helium. This is a nuclear reaction that releases huge amounts of energy.

WHITE DWARF

The sun will eventually become a RED GIANT.

Death of a star

It is estimated that in about 5 billion years, the outer part of the sun will get bigger and cooler. The sun will turn into a type of star called a red giant. Finally, outer layers will drift away, leaving a small central core called a white dwarf.

A sundial

A sundial is a simple kind of clock (right). You can make your own sundial by sticking some clay in the middle of a large circle of cardboard and pushing a pencil into the clay. Put the sundial in a sunny place and mark where the shadow falls each hour.

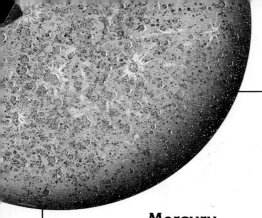

THE INNER PLANETS

The inner planets – Mercury, Venus, Earth, and Mars – are the four planets that are closest to the sun. They are also called the rocky planets, because each one is made of rock and metal. Although they are all different sizes, the inner planets are much smaller than the giant gas planets, Jupiter and Saturn.

Mercury

Mercury is the closest planet to the sun. There is no atmosphere or water on Mercury, and it is bathed in fiery heat and light from the sun. Its surface is covered with craters.

Venus

The atmosphere on Venus is made of carbon dioxide gas, and there are thick clouds of sulfuric acid. On the surface there are probably deep cracks and active volcanoes.

When seen from space, the EARTH looks like a blue ball with white clouds swirling around it. •

Mars

Most of Mars is covered with red rocks and dust. If you look at Mars through a telescope, you will see white patches at the top and bottom. These are the planet's polar ice-caps (right), which are like the frozen North and South Poles on earth. Mars also has craters and huge, extinct volcanoes.

Earth

Earth is the only planet in the solar system where we know that life definitely exists. Living things can survive on earth because our planet has liquid water, air that we can breathe, and comfortable temperatures. No other planet in the solar system has these three things.

Aliens

Do you believe that there is life beyond our solar system? What do you think creatures from outer space might look like? A being from another planet is often referred to as an alien. Books and films like *E.T.* have tried to show how aliens from space might look. Use your imagination to draw your own alien from outer space.

THE GIANT PLANETS

Jupiter and Saturn are the two largest and fastest-spinning planets in the solar system. They spin around so quickly that each one bulges at its equator. Both planets are huge balls of liquid and gas, and neither has a solid surface so no spacecraft can land there. However, an American space probe may land on one of Saturn's moons soon after the year 2000.

Jupiter

Jupiter is so huge that it contains more material than all the other planets put together. Fierce storms and colored bands of clouds swirl around the surface. The Great Red Spot on Jupiter's surface is a huge, spinning storm cloud.

SATURN'S RINGS are made of millions of pieces of ice and dust.

Jupiter's GREAT RED SPOT spins in a counter-clockwise direction.

JUPITER was the king of all the Roman gods.

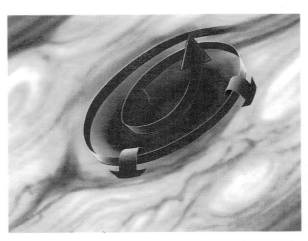

Saturn

Like Jupiter, Saturn is another giant ball of gas. Its center is surrounded by many shining rings. Each ring is made up of thousands of smaller ringlets. Saturn has at least 18 moons. The largest one, Titan, is even bigger than the planet Mercury.

The VOYAGER space probes carry records called "Sounds on Earth" in case they are ever picked up by alien life.

Planet names

MARS

Did you know that the planets are named after the gods of the ancient Greeks and Romans? Jupiter was the king of all the Roman gods, Mars was the god of war and Mercury, the god of roads and travel, was also the messenger of the gods. The Roman god of agriculture was Saturn. Can you find out who the other planets were named after?

MERCURY

THE OUTER PLANETS

The three planets that are farthest away from the sun are Uranus, Neptune, and Pluto. Uranus and Neptune are giant balls of gas. But the gases that make up Pluto are frozen because the planet is so far away from the sun's heat. For most of the time, Pluto is the planet that lies farthest from the sun. You need a telescope to see these three planets.

The space probe Voyager 2 discovered eleven thin RINGS around the center of Uranus.

TITANIA

OBERON

Uranus

The planet Uranus was discovered in 1781 by the English astronomer Sir William Herschel. Uranus is odd because it is tilted in such a way that it spins on its side as it orbits the sun. It is made up of a small, rocky core and frozen gases, surrounded by greenish-blue clouds. Titania, Oberon, and Puck are three of Uranus' fifteen moons.

PUCK

Famous astronomers

The ancient Greek astronomer, Ptolemy, believed that the sun and the planets traveled around the earth. In 1543, a Polish monk called Copernicus said that the sun, and not the earth, was at the center of the Universe. The Italian astronomer, Galileo (right), was probably the first person to study the night sky using a telescope.

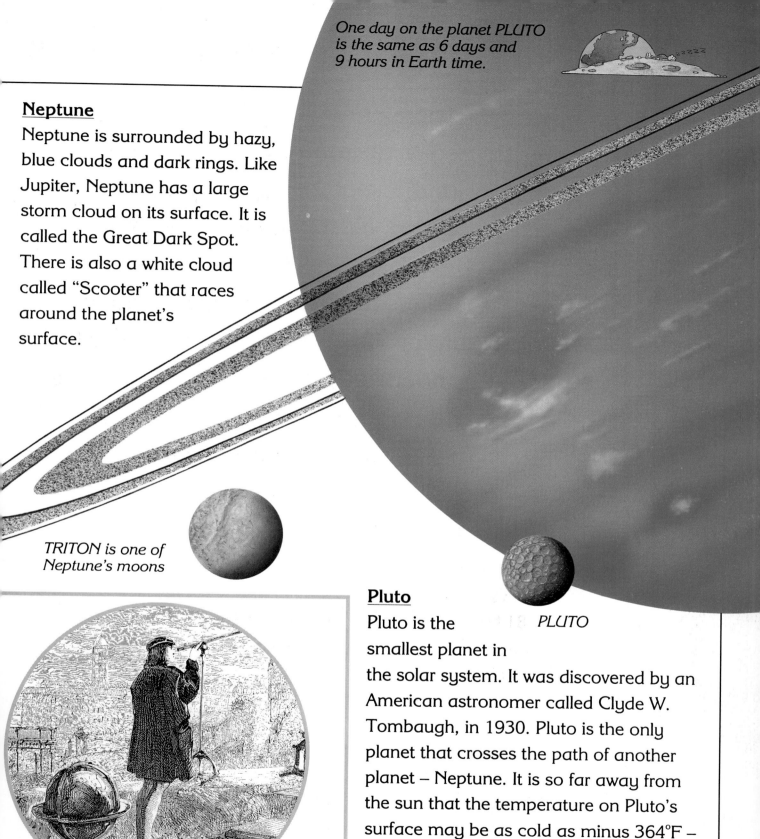

One day on the planet PLUTO is the same as 6 days and 9 hours in Earth time.

Neptune

Neptune is surrounded by hazy, blue clouds and dark rings. Like Jupiter, Neptune has a large storm cloud on its surface. It is called the Great Dark Spot. There is also a white cloud called "Scooter" that races around the planet's surface.

TRITON is one of Neptune's moons

PLUTO

Pluto

Pluto is the smallest planet in the solar system. It was discovered by an American astronomer called Clyde W. Tombaugh, in 1930. Pluto is the only planet that crosses the path of another planet – Neptune. It is so far away from the sun that the temperature on Pluto's surface may be as cold as minus 364°F – that's more than twice as cold as the coldest place on earth.

MOONS

There are at least 60 moons in the solar system. The most studied moon, and one of the largest, is the Earth's moon. Most planets have one or more moons – Saturn has 18. Mercury and Venus are the only two planets in the solar system that do not have any moons at all.

What is an eclipse?

An eclipse of the sun (above) happens when the moon passes in front of the sun, blocking off its light from the Earth. Eclipses of the moon are much more common. They happen when the Earth comes between the sun and the moon, so that the moon is in the Earth's shadow.

The Man in the Moon

Have you heard of the Man in the Moon? Some people think that the dark patches on the moon's surface look like the face of a man. Others believe they can see a beautiful woman, a cat, a rabbit, and even a frog. What shapes can you see when you look up at the moon?

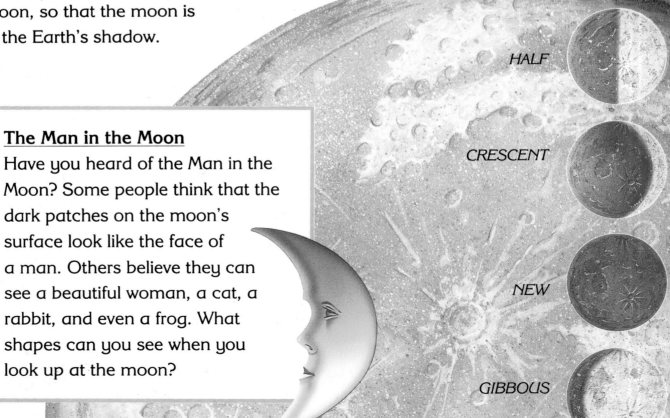

FULL

HALF

CRESCENT

NEW

GIBBOUS

EUROPA

CALLISTO

TITAN

IO

GANYMEDE

Natural satellites

Satellites are objects that travel around a larger object. A moon is a natural satellite that orbits a planet. Titan is by far the largest of Saturn's 18 moons, and is unusual because it has its own atmosphere. Jupiter's moons are also unusual because they have different surfaces. Io is very rocky and has active volcanoes, but Europa is smooth and icy. Callisto's surface is covered with thousands of craters. Ganymede, the largest moon in the solar system, has craters and deep grooves hundreds of miles long.

*MIMAS is one of
Saturn's 18 moons.*

The Earth's moon

We know more about our moon than any other place in the solar system (apart from the Earth). The moon is made of rock and has no air or water. On its surface, there are hills, mountains, flat plains, and craters. From the Earth, the moon appears to change shape (left). These are called "phases," and happen because we only see the sunlit part of the moon as it orbits the Earth.

SHOOTING STARS

Shooting stars are not really stars at all. They are streaks of light that appear in the night sky. Another name for a shooting star is a meteor. They are made when pieces of rock, iron, and dust from space burn up in the Earth's atmosphere, producing streaks of light.

Meteorites

Meteorites are pieces of space rock and iron that actually land on the Earth's surface. This happens because they are too big to burn up completely in the Earth's atmosphere. Large meteorites, which landed on Earth thousands of years ago, created huge dents, called craters.

When ASTEROIDS collide, pieces of rock and iron break off.

Meteor showers

When the Earth passes through a dust trail left by a comet (see page 20), we see a meteor shower. In 1966, up to 46,000 meteors appeared in the night sky in just twenty minutes. It was one of the largest meteor showers ever seen.

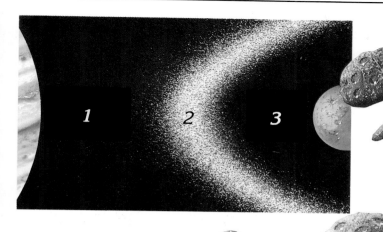

1
2
3

These are just some of the thousands of asteroids in the ASTEROID BELT.

1 JUPITER
2 ASTEROID BELT
3 MARS

CERES

What is the asteroid belt?

Large rocks that orbit the sun are called asteroids. Asteroids are found in a part of the solar system that is known as the asteroid belt. It lies between Mars and Jupiter, and contains more than 4,000 asteroids. Ceres, which is the largest asteroid, measures nearly 560 miles across.

Looking at telescopes

We use telescopes to see very faint things that are far away in space. A telescope collects light from an object, for example a planet, and then makes the image of that planet bigger. Reflecting telescopes have curved mirrors to collect light. The first reflecting telescope was made by Sir Isaac Newton, the famous English scientist, in 1669.

One of the largest meteor CRATERS is in Arizona. It is more than half a mile wide and 574 feet deep.

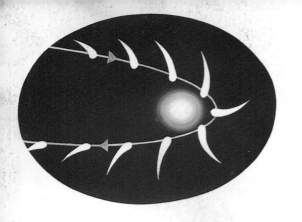

WHAT ARE COMETS?

Comets are found in the farthest parts of the solar system. They are like huge, dirty snowballs. Scientists think that there may be millions of comets up in space. Some comets have long orbits and take hundreds, or even thousands, of years to travel around the sun.

A comet's tail
Behind or sometimes in front of the comet's head streams a long tail of dust and gas. The tail always points away from the sun. As comets travel toward the sun, they grow larger.

Halley's comet
One of the best-known comets is named after the English astronomer Edmond Halley. He first saw it in 1682. Halley's comet takes 76 years to orbit the sun. It was last seen from earth in 1986 and is due to return in the year 2062.

In 1986, the space probe GIOTTO sent back many new pictures of Halley's comet.

EDMOND HALLEY

The Bayeux Tapestry

The Bayeux Tapestry is a very long piece of linen on which many colorful pictures have been embroidered. It tells the story of how the Normans from France invaded and conquered England in 1066. In one of the tapestry's pictures, a comet can be seen in the sky. Some scientists believe that it must have been Halley's comet.

The nucleus

The center, or nucleus, of a comet contains ice, frozen gases, and pieces of rock and dust. As the comet gets closer to the sun, a cloud of gases forms around the nucleus. Although the nucleus is often only a few miles wide, the cloud of gases might measure more than one million miles across.

OUTER CRUST

NUCLEUS

ICE

EXPLORING THE SOLAR SYSTEM

Hundreds of spacecraft have been launched to explore the solar system. Most of them do not carry astronauts (left) and are controlled by robots and computers. These unmanned spacecraft are called probes. Some fly past distant planets and send back pictures to earth. Others actually land on the planets to collect rock samples or to study the weather conditions.

Humans in space

The first person walked on the moon's surface in July 1969. He was an American astronaut named Neil Armstrong.

URANUS
1986

The VOYAGER 2 space probe has traveled over 4.35 billion miles in space. On its journey, it has taken pictures of Jupiter, Saturn, Uranus (above), and Neptune.

NEPTUNE
1989

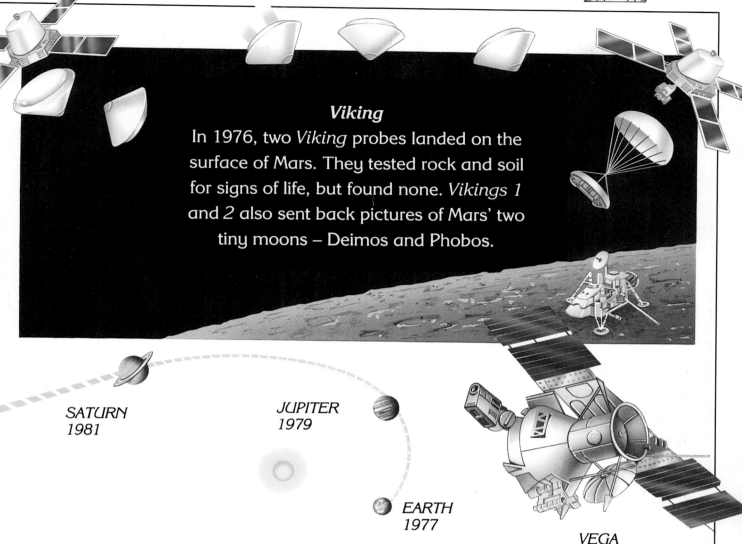

Viking
In 1976, two *Viking* probes landed on the surface of Mars. They tested rock and soil for signs of life, but found none. *Vikings 1* and *2* also sent back pictures of Mars' two tiny moons – Deimos and Phobos.

SATURN
1981

JUPITER
1979

EARTH
1977

VEGA

Make a balloon rocket
Blow up a long balloon and tape its neck tightly. Tape a straw to the balloon and thread a piece of nylon cord through it. Tie each end to a piece of furniture. Undo the neck and watch your rocket fly!

Space probes
The first probe to reach a planet was *Mariner 2*, which flew close to Venus in 1962. More than 20 years later, the Soviet probes *Vega 1* and *2* dropped weather balloons into Venus' atmosphere. Two *Pioneer* and two *Voyager* probes are traveling to the edge of the solar system to explore what lies beyond Pluto.

THE NIGHT SKY

What can you see?

Venus is by far the brightest planet in the sky. It looks like a bright star, and is called the "evening star" at sunset, or the "morning star" at sunrise. Mars is often called the "Red Planet" because of its reddish color. You can often see these planets with your naked eye. However, you will see much more detail if you use binoculars or a telescope.

Do you know how to find the planets in the sky at night? First, you must choose a clear, dark night for watching the sky. You will see hundreds of twinkling stars, but among them are the planets. They shine with a steadier light than the stars because they are much closer to the earth. The easiest planets to spot are Venus, Mars, Jupiter, and Saturn.

SATURN

MARS

VENUS

MOON

Star shapes

Groups of stars form shapes in the night sky, called constellations. North of the Equator, the clearest constellations are the Great Bear (right) and Orion the Hunter (left). Three bright stars make up Orion's belt. South of the Equator, four bright stars form the famous Southern Cross, or Crux, constellation. You can also see Orion and the Great Bear, but they appear upside down.

PLANET FACTS

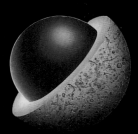

MERCURY
Distance from sun:
36 million miles
Diameter: 3,032 miles
Number of moons: 0
Length of a year:
88 Earth days
Structure: Ball of rock
with a core of iron
Temperature range:
−279°F to 800°F

VENUS
Distance from sun:
67 million miles
Diameter: 7,519 miles
Number of moons: 0
Length of a year: 225
Earth days
Structure: Rocky
planet with metal core
rich in iron
Temperature: 896° F

EARTH
Distance from sun: 93
million miles
Diameter: 7,926 miles
Number of moons: 1
Length of a year: 365
Earth days
Structure: Metallic core,
surrounded by rock
Temperature range:
−130°F to 136°F

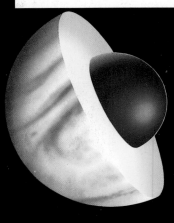

- SUN
- MERCURY
- VENUS
- EARTH
- MARS
- ASTEROID BELT
- JUPITER
- SATURN
- URANUS
- NEPTUNE
- PLUTO

MARS
Distance from sun:
142 million miles
Diameter: 4,194 miles
Number of moons: 2
Length of a year: 687
Earth days
Structure: Rocky ball
with a core rich in iron
Temperature range:
−266°F to -62°F

JUPITER
Distance from sun: 483
million miles
Diameter: 88,736 miles
Number of moons: 16
Length of a year: 4,333
Earth days
Structure: Small rocky
core surrounded by
liquid and gases
Temperature: −278°F

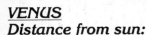

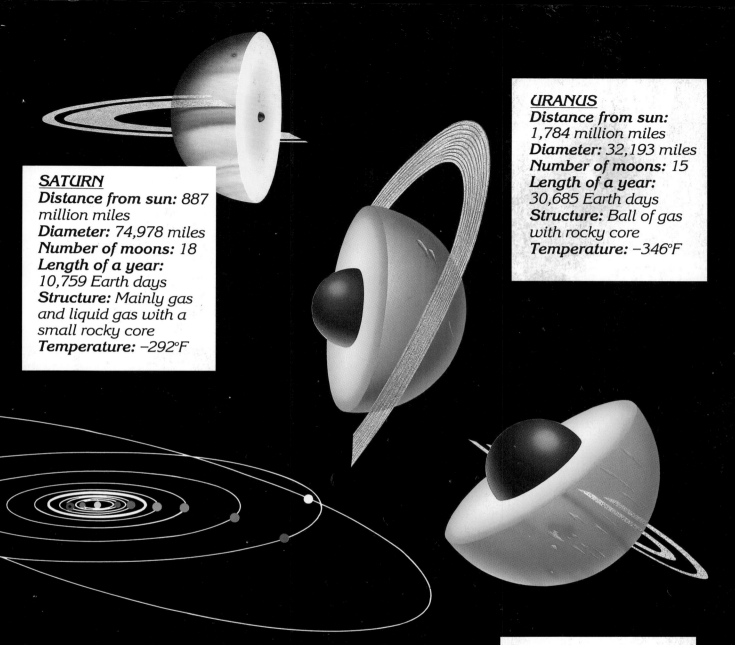

SATURN
Distance from sun: 887 million miles
Diameter: 74,978 miles
Number of moons: 18
Length of a year: 10,759 Earth days
Structure: Mainly gas and liquid gas with a small rocky core
Temperature: −292°F

URANUS
Distance from sun: 1,784 million miles
Diameter: 32,193 miles
Number of moons: 15
Length of a year: 30,685 Earth days
Structure: Ball of gas with rocky core
Temperature: −346°F

NEPTUNE
Distance from sun: 2,796 million miles
Diameter: 30,775 miles
Number of moons: 8
Length of a year: 60,190 Earth days
Structure: Ball of gas with metal core
Temperature: −353°F

PLUTO
Distance from sun: 3,666 million miles
Diameter: 1,423 miles
Number of moons: 1
Length of a year: 90,800 Earth days
Structure: Ball of rock and ice
Temperature: approx. −364°F

A SOLAR SYSTEM QUIZ

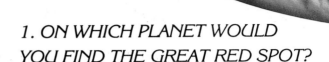

How much do you know about the solar system? Can you remember what a shooting star is? And which planet has 18 moons orbiting around it? Here is a solar system quiz to test how much you have learned. The picture clues should help you to find the right answers. You could try out the quiz on your friends or other people in your family. All the answers can be found on the pages of this book.

1. ON WHICH PLANET WOULD YOU FIND THE GREAT RED SPOT?

2. WHERE IS THE ASTEROID BELT?

3. WHICH SPACECRAFT SENT BACK NEW PICTURES OF HALLEY'S COMET IN 1986?

4. WHO WAS THE FIRST PERSON TO WALK ON THE MOON?

5. WHAT IS THE NAME OF THIS CONSTELLATION?

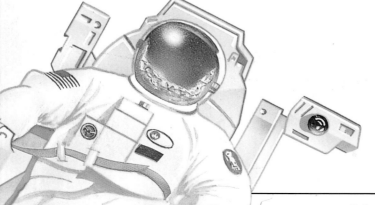

6. WHAT IS THE NAME OF OUR GALAXY ?

7. WHAT IS A
RED GIANT?

9. WHICH IS THE SMALLEST PLANET
IN THE SOLAR SYSTEM?

8. WHICH PLANET IS NAMED
AFTER THE ROMAN GOD OF
AGRICULTURE?

MORE FASCINATING FACTS

The world's largest OPTICAL TELESCOPE, in Hawaii, is 200 million times more powerful than the human eye.

The temperature on VENUS is more than 8 times hotter than at the hottest places on Earth.

The whole state of Maryland could fit inside the BAILLY CRATER, the largest crater on the moon.

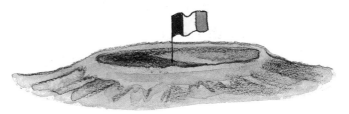

SATURN is so light that it could float in water.

The "SEAS" on the moon are really flat areas of dark rock and contain no water at all.

A Japanese construction company is planning to build a HOTEL in space by the year 2020.

The longest measured ECLIPSE of the sun, in June 1955, lasted 7 minutes and 8 seconds.

GLOSSARY

ASTEROID A rocky object in the solar system that orbits the sun. Often called "minor planet."

ATMOSPHERE The mixture of gases that surrounds a planet.

CONSTELLATION A group of stars forming a pattern in the night sky. Because the Earth spins around, constellations seem to move across the sky each night.

CORE The central part of a planet.

CRATER A large dent on the surface of a planet or a moon.

EQUATOR An imaginary line around the middle of a planet.

GALAXY A huge family of stars, planets, and other objects in space.

METEOR A streak of light in the night sky caused by a piece of rock or iron burning up in the Earth's atmosphere. Also called "shooting star."

METEORITE A piece of space rock or metal that lands on the Earth's surface.

MILKY WAY The huge galaxy of stars that includes the solar system. On a dark night it can be seen as a faint band of light across the sky.

NUCLEUS The central part of a comet's head.

ORBIT To move around another object in space.

PLANET A large object in space that travels around the sun.

PROBE An unmanned spacecraft that explores space.

RED GIANT A huge star whose fuel supply has almost run out.

SATELLITE An object in space that moves around a planet, a moon, or a spacecraft.

STAR A very bright ball of gas that gives out lots of heat and light. The sun is a star.

UNIVERSE Everything that exists – including the solar system, the Milky Way and all the other galaxies in space.

INDEX

PHOTOCREDITS

page 11 bottom: Frank Spooner Pictures; page 15 bottom: Mary Evans Picture Library.

PRINTED IN BELGIUM BY
INTERNATIONAL BOOK PRODUCTION